D1390417

CONTRACT BRIDGE IN 20 MINUTES

CONTRACT BRIDGE IN 20 MINUTES

BY

HAROLD THORNE

WITH AN INTRODUCTION BY

ELY CULBERTSON

CHIEF EDITOR, "THE BRIDGE WORLD MAGAZINE"

LONDON

EYRE & SPOTTISWOODE

6 GREAT NEW STREET, E.C. 4

First Edition . . . December 1930
Second Edition . . . . January 1931
Third Edition . . . February 1931
Fourth Edition . . . . . April 1931
Fifth Edition . . . August 1931
Sixth Edition . . . November 1931
Seventh Edition . . . November 1931
Eighth Edition . . . February 1932
Ninth Edition . . . February 1932
Tenth Edition . . . . . May 1932
Eleventh Edition . . September 1932

Printed in Great Britain for
Eyre and Spottiswoode (Publishers) Limited, London

INTRODUCTION

MR. THORNE'S little book is a splendid starting-off place for beginners, not only in Contract but in Auction. For those who have a fair idea of Auction this manual will be a most convenient bridge to cross to the more alluring and perplexing camp of Contract. This bridge is also safe, for Mr. Thorne is particularly careful to explain not so much the ideas and idiosyncrasies of a single writer as to point out the general direction of to-day's Contract which it will no doubt follow in the future.

The Forcing System of Contract is already played by the overwhelming majority of leading experts and clubs and adopted by most writers. This simple but precise system is based entirely upon natural inferences. To the average player or beginner it will be a great help because it will enable anyone to play a winning game regardless of system used by either partner or adversaries.

What particularly pleases me is that the book, in spite of its modest size, is complete and includes practically all the departments of the game. Unfortunately this cannot be said about many books five times the size and ten times the price.

ELY CULBERTSON,
Chief Editor,
The Bridge World Magazine.

45 West 45th Street,
New York City.

PREFACE

In endeavouring to write a simple and clear description of present-day "CONTRACT," the author has studied most of the leading works by the various stars of the Contract Bridge firmament, and has endeavoured to concentrate the best features of the different authorities, especially the "Forcing System" as outlined by its originator, Mr. Ely Culbertson, chief editor of *The Bridge World Magazine*. If the reader should prefer any particular method, he can readily secure a more detailed account by purchasing one of the many books now on the market.

In valuing the hands, Mr. Culbertson uses a method of counting "HONOUR TRICKS." Mr. Whitehead uses a method of counting "QUICK TRICKS." Mr. Work uses a method of counting honours for bidding No Trumps.

The definition of an "HONOUR TRICK" is a trick that will be taken by an honour.

The definition of a "QUICK TRICK" is a trick that will probably be made on the first or second lead of the suit.

Mr. Work counts an Ace as four, King as three, Queen as two, and Jack as one. With no suit bid, but holding a count of thirteen, bid one No Trump; holding count of seventeen, bid two; twenty-one, bid three. The assisting hand, with count of nine, raises partner's one bid to two; with count of thirteen, raise one bid to three. With count of six, raise two bid to three.

CONTRACT BRIDGE IN 20 MINUTES

NOTE

THIS book will give the average card-player an up-to-date working knowledge of Contract Bridge in the short time of 20 minutes.

Fifteen pages, numbered from three to seventeen, contain " the meat in the cocoanut." The remaining pages are devoted to general information.

There are ten important things to remember, each clearly marked and numbered.

THE MAIN DIFFERENCES BETWEEN CONTRACT AND AUCTION BRIDGE

1st. Only tricks bid and made can be scored below the line in contract. All extra tricks are scored in the honour column.

2nd. The trick values are three times as high as in auction and the penalties are heavier if doubled, particularly after one game has been made.

3rd. The bidding is practically the same, excepting that one must bear in mind that only tricks bid and made can be scored below the line.

4th. No premiums are allowed for slams unless bid and made. With no game scored the premium for a small slam is 500, for grand slam 1000. If game has previously been made, then side having game is termed vulnerable and slam premiums are increased to 750 for small slam and 1500 for grand slam.

5th. The only honours scored are four or five in one hand. Four scores 100 points; five, 150 points. Four aces in one hand, 150 points.

NOTE: The premiums for slams are large, but

it is useless to keep shooting at the moon unless you have the ammunition.

<table>
<tr><td>REMEMBER
No. 1</td><td>Always look at the score before bidding.
It is most important to play the hand in the most suitable suit</td></tr>
</table>

for the two hands, and only by safe and sane bidding by partners working as a team can such an object be achieved.

BIDDING

There has been a general idea that it is inadvisable for beginners to bid four-card suits. Practice has established the fact that frequently a four-card suit is the best opening bid, and it is advisable for beginners to start in the proper path and learn to bid correctly.

For example of a four-card suit bid, see page 6.

An *original* or *opening* bid is the *first* bid made.

It is absolutely necessary to know the true value of the hand, and an easy way to acquire this knowledge is to count the honour tricks.

HONOUR TRICKS TABLE.
(Should be memorized.)

½ Trick	1 Trick
Any K x	Any Ace
Any Q J x	Any K Q x
(Q x and J x in	Any K J x
different suits,	(K x and Q x in
have some value)	different suits,
	have some value)

1½ Tricks
Any A Q   2 Tricks   2½ Tricks
Any A J 10   A K   A K Q
Any K Q 10

Example :

Spades :   King, 8, 2 (½ Trick)
Hearts :   Ace, Queen, 6 (1½ Tricks)

Diamonds : King, Queen, 4, 2 (1 Trick)
Clubs :   Queen, Jack, 4 (½ Trick)

The values given are *defensive minimum* which should take tricks even against opponents' trump bids. For this reason honour combinations like A K Q, A K J, K Q J, A Q 10, which at own or partner's bid are worth somewhat more, must be valued at the minimum defensive basis.

NOTE: On the average, eight of the thirteen tricks will be taken with honours.

BIDDING "ONE NO-TRUMP"

Holding two and a half honour tricks in three suits, with no suit bid, bid " one no-trump."

ORIGINAL BIDS OF A SUIT

Holding one and a half honour tricks in two outside suits, and at least four trumps with three honours (or ace-queen, or king-queen), bid one of suit.

Example (1st or 2nd hand bid):

Spades :	K Q 9 6	Equals 1 Trick
Hearts :	A 7 6	Equals 1 Trick
Diamonds :	K J 10	Equals 1 Trick
Clubs :	7 6 5	Total 3 Tricks

Bid " One Spade "

Beginners like to bid long suits without honours. With a six-card suit containing one honour and two outside honour tricks, bid one of the suit.

Bidding *third* hand requires half a trick more.

An *original suit bid of three* indicates that the hand is best played in that suit, and that declarer is not so particular about the number of trumps in dummy, and that the hand holds at least eight tricks, if played in suit named.

Example :

Spades :	A K Q 10 9 7	Equals 5 Tricks
Hearts :	A K	Equals 2 Tricks
Diamonds :	K Q	Equals 1 Trick
Clubs :	x x x	Total 8 Tricks

> REMEMBER
> NO. 2

An *original* suit bid of *two* indicates a stronger hand than an *original* suit bid of *three*. It shows five honour tricks in *three* suits and demands, *unconditionally*, that partner keep the bidding open. Declarer may or may not have an alternative bid or slam material. It is called a forcing bid, originated by Mr. Culbertson.

Example : Original two-bid hand :

Spades :	A Q 9 3 2	Equals 1½ Tricks
Hearts :	A K 10 7 3	Equals 2 Tricks
Diamonds :	A	Equals 1 Trick
Clubs :	K x	Equals ½ Trick
		Total 5 Tricks

[7]

REPLYING TO PARTNER'S BID OF ONE NO TRUMP

With less than $1\frac{1}{2}$ tricks—" Pass."

With any five-card suit headed by Queen, Ten or better, and $1\frac{1}{2}$ to 2 honour tricks, bid two of suit.

With good five-card suit and three honour tricks or more, jump bid to three of suit (forcing bid). Partner will keep bidding open. (If without trump help, by bidding " three no-trumps "—With trump help, by bidding four of suit.)

REPLYING TO SUIT BID OF ONE

To assist partner's bid of one, you are expected to have four small trumps, or three with Queen or better, and two assisting tricks; holding this, raise the bid to two.

Example : Partner bid " One Spade." You hold :

Spades :	x x x x	
Hearts :	K Q	1 Trick
Diamonds :	A x x	1 Trick
Clubs :	x x x x	Total 2 Tricks

Raise Bid to " Two Spades "

For each additional assisting trick, increase the bid by one trick; that is, holding the trumps as aforementioned, and four assisting tricks, jump the bid to four. (With trump ability—at least three small—a missing suit is worth two tricks, a singleton, one trick. With four trumps, a missing suit is worth three, singleton two, doubleton one.)

REMEMBER No. 3

Watch the score. Do not increase the bid unnecessarily unless you are going for a slam. Not holding the required number of trumps, and having a weak hand (less than $1\frac{1}{2}$ honour tricks), pass. Your partner will understand that you are denying the suit. Unlike Auction, in Contract one does not deny a suit by mentioning another, the act of passing is a denial.

Example : Partner has bid " One Spade." You hold :

Spades :   x x x   Diamonds : J x x x
Hearts : K J x   Clubs :   x x x

" Pass "

Changing partner's suit to " no-trumps." Holding some small cards of your partner's suit and

the other three suits stopped, bid a " no-trump."
Your partner will exercise care in advancing such
a bid.

Example : Partner bid " One Spade." You
hold :

Spades : x x x	Diamonds : K 10 8
Hearts : J 10 8	Clubs : A x x x

Bid " One No-Trump "

Changing partner's bid to another suit. Having a
suit of five or more, containing at least one honour
trick, and holding at least half an honour trick
in another suit, bid your suit. This is termed a
non-forcing take-out.

Example : Partner has bid " One Spade." You
hold :

Spades : x x	Diamonds : Q J x
Hearts : K J x x x	Clubs : x x x

Bid " Two Hearts "

A forcing take-out, originated by Mr. Culbertson,
is one of the most important features of Contract. Such

a take-out may indicate game or slam at some bid.

Example : Partner has bid " One Heart." You hold :

Spades : A K Q 10 7   Diamonds : K Q x x x
Hearts : x x   Clubs :   A

Bid " Two Spades " (Forcing Bid)

Any jump bid in some *other suit, below game Contract,* is a forcing bid and demands that opening hand shall *unconditionally* keep the bidding open. A *forcing take-out* may indicate an even better hand than the opening bid. It shows at least three honour tricks and a good five-card suit. The *compulsory* "minimum response" is the " no-trump " bid, so termed because it does not increase the contract.

Assisting a suit bid of three. Regardless of trumps, with one assisting trick, raise to four. Raise to five with three honour tricks in the other suits.

Assisting a suit bid of two. Holding four small trumps, or three including Queen or better, and one assisting trick, raise to three. With the trumps and two assisting tricks, raise to four. With four honour tricks, raise to five. Having weakness in partner's bid, name any five-card suit. Holding " nothing," give " minimum raise " of two no-trumps.

THE INFORMATIVE DOUBLE

Of a suit bid of one or two, or a "*one* no-trump " bid :

It frequently happens that opponents bid a suit in which you are weak, but you hold strength in the other three suits and would prefer to hear from your partner as to which of these three suits is best fitted to his hand. To compel your partner to answer this question, the informatory double was invented.

Example : Opponents bid " One Heart." You hold :

Spades : A Q 10   Diamonds : K J 8 4
Hearts : x x   Clubs :   K Q x x

You " Double One Heart." Your partner is compelled to answer the double by bidding something, preferably a suit.

REPLYING TO INFORMATIVE DOUBLE

Having no suit bid, but strength in the suit doubled, bid "no-trumps." Partner will bear in mind that the bid was compulsory. Having a legitimate bid, answer the double by jumping the bid.

REMEMBER No. 4	An intervening bid absolves you from bidding. Should you then bid, it indicates great strength in the suit named.

REMEMBER No. 5	The double is only informatory when used at the first opportunity, and when the doubler's partner has not bid a suit or

" no-trump " or doubled.

A double of " *two* no-trumps " is a business double.

BUSINESS DOUBLES

Care should be exercised in doubling. It is inexcusable for the opponents to be doubled into making game.

Avoid doubling if opponents can switch to a safer suit.

REMEMBER No. 6 — Be careful in considering strength in a suit that has been bid by opponent on your left. Holding the ace counts, holding King, Queen and two others, or King, Jack, Ten and another are even better than Ace. Such holdings as King and two others, or Queen and two should not be considered.

LEADING TO A SUIT BID

Remember the bidding and try and place the cards in the various hands. If your partner has bid, lead the highest of his suit unless you have four or more, then lead fourth best. Holding an unmentioned suit headed by Ace, King, lead the King, then your partner's suit. Your partner will then know how to get back into your hand when necessary.

Holding Ace, King only, lead Ace.

Holding Ace, King, Queen, lead King, then Queen.

Holding Ace, King and another, lead King.

REMEMBER No. 7	Lead through the strong suits in dummy, that is, make dummy play second hand with its strong suits. In leading up to dummy,

lead up to weakness; that is, make dummy play fourth hand with its weak suits.

Top of nothing was considered a good lead. It is not. Lead middle card of three-card suit. Your partner may or may not return it.

Avoid opening a suit headed by ace; if compulsory, lead ace.

Never lead away from an Ace, Queen, wait until it is led to you unless your partner has indicated a high card in the suit by the informatory discard of a six or better.

Unless you have some particular reason, avoid leading away from a King.

REMEMBER No. 8	Do not lead a singleton unless you have the trumps stopped. Other authorities to the contrary notwithstanding, usually the lead

of a singleton sets up the suit, your opponent draws the trumps, and discards a lot of losing cards on the suit that you have aided to establish.

Avoid leading a doubleton. It is a rotten lead, but sometimes advisable.

Never lead a suit which declarer can trump in either hand, declarer invariably discards a losing card.

<table>
<tr><td>REMEMBER No. 9</td><td>It is frequently good business to make the declarer trump in his own hand.</td></tr>
</table>

<table>
<tr><td>REMEMBER No. 10</td><td>It is often advisable to lead to a positive trick in dummy, rather than open a new suit through your partner.</td></tr>
</table>

FINESSING

Don't unless necessary, but if you are obliged to do so the following are points to remember :

Lead small card up to Ace, Queen.

With Ace x x in one hand and Queen x x in the other, lead small towards Queen. Never Queen towards Ace.

With Ace x x and Queen, Ten x in the other, take with the Ace and lead small ; if second hand plays low, play Ten, if Jack is in second hand the Ten will call the King.

With Ace, Jack x in one hand, and King, Ten x in the other, wait until opponents lead that suit and you will make three tricks.

Holding Queen, Jack, Ten in one hand and Ace x x in the other, lead Queen towards Ace.

Having Ace, Jack, Ten in one hand, lead from the other hand and beat second hand's card.

With Ace, Queen in one hand and King located on the left, throw the lead in that hand on the eleventh trick.

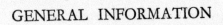

GENERAL INFORMATION

TWO-SUITED HANDS

Two-suited hands are the best and easiest to play. They should hold at least two and a half honour tricks. If of equal value, bid the higher ranking first. Bid a five-card minor containing half a trick, before bidding a four-card major. Show the second suit at the earliest possible moment, unless your partner has supported your first bid.

Mentioning higher ranking first gives your partner the opportunity of selecting the better suit without increasing the contract.

If not of equal value, bid the better suit first, as, if an intervening bid prevents mention of your second suit, your partner will at least have been informed of the best suit for defence.

SLAM BIDDING

The bidding having been carried high enough to score game, any Voluntary increase is a Slam Invitation.

The old idea of showing Aces is no longer considered sound.

It is still good play, when desirable, to show

Ace or Chicane of opponents' suit by overbidding opponents in their own suit. This is a forcing bid and shows at least three tricks.

THE VANDERBILT CONVENTION

This convention was quite popular at one time. The idea was to inform your partner that you held three Quick Tricks and were open to suggestions. This was accomplished by bidding one Club. Such a bid held no suggestion that any of the Quick Tricks were in the Club suit. Not having two Quick Tricks, the reply should be a bid of one Diamond, which bid in no way implied that the hand held Diamonds. Having a strong hand, bid accordingly.

BUSINESS DOUBLE

When your partner has doubled (Business), do not take him out of the double unless you have misled him as to the Honour Tricks in your hand or hold a freak hand of which he was not previously informed.

REDOUBLING A BUSINESS DOUBLE

Redoubling a business double is good business if you are certain of making your contract, and know that there is no suit to which your opponents may switch.

LEADING NO-TRUMPS BID

Opponents have bid "No-Trumps." Your lead, and partner has not bid. Lead fourth best of your longest suit. By the "RULE OF ELEVEN" your partner will be able to locate nearly all the cards of the suit.

RULE OF ELEVEN

Deduct the number of the card led from eleven, and the result will tell the number of better cards held against leader. *Example :* A six spot is led. Six from eleven leaves five. There are five cards higher than the one led and none of the five held by leader. There may be two in your hand and two in Dummy—if so, fourth hand can only have one card better than the six.

UNBLOCKING

Be careful not to block your partner's suit. That is, do not keep a final high card of his suit in your hand, as you may have some difficulty in getting the lead back to him. If he led the Ace, it calls for your highest card—he wants to know where the high cards are.

In following to partner's lead when not attempting to take the trick—having three of the suit,

[23]

play second highest, then highest. Having only two, play highest.

OPPONENTS OVERCALLING PARTNER'S " NO-TRUMP " BID

Having opponents' suit stopped twice and one probable trick, raise your partner's bid one trick. With the suit stopped twice and two probable tricks, raise partner's bid two tricks.

GOULASHES

THERE ARE SEVERAL FORMS. NONE LEGAL.

After all four players have passed, the various hands should be arranged in suits and graded. Dealer places his hand on the table—Player on the right places his hand on top of Dealer's—Dealer's partner next—Person on left of Dealer last. Cards are then straightened up and cut. Dealer deals five at a time twice around, then three. A penalty of 100 points is claimed for a misdeal.

GOULASHES are OPTIONAL. If ONE player objects, Goulashes cannot be played.

Sometimes cards are exchanged between partners. The usual procedure is to exchange three, then two, and finally one. A singleton in the first three indicates the suit required. If the singleton is a six or better, it indicates that partner holds the Ace.

Exchanging one, then three, and two, is another form. First card passed shows suit desired. If a high honour is passed, return it. If both partners desire the same suit, the player receiving the highest honour keeps it.

Frequently it is agreed that if one side is vulnerable, both sides shall be considered so.

In Goulashes ONLY, the lead of a King denies the Ace.

EXAMPLE OF FORCING BIDS

<pre>
                Spades :   10
                Hearts :   K 10 3 2
                Diamonds :   J 8 7 2
                Clubs :   J 7 6 2
Spades :   Q 8 5   ┌─────────┐   Spades :   J 7 6 4
Hearts :   5 4   │   N   │   Hearts :   J 6
Diamonds : 9 6 5 4 │ W   E │   Diamonds : A Q 10
Clubs :   K 10 4 3 │   S   │   Clubs :   Q 9 8 5
                     └─────────┘
                Spades :   A K 9 3 2
                Hearts :   A Q 9 8 7
                Diamonds :   K 3
                Clubs :   A
</pre>

No score. South dealt and holding five tricks bids " Two Spades " (Forcing Bid). West passes. North " Two No Trumps " (minimum raise, keeping bidding open). East passes. South then bids " Three Hearts "—West passes—North bids " Four Hearts."

EXAMPLE OF FORCING TAKE-OUT

<pre>
              Spades :   10
              Hearts :   3
              Diamonds : A 10 7 6
              Clubs :   A K Q J 7 6 2
Spades :   Q 8 5   ┌───────┐   Spades :   J 7 6 4
Hearts :   10 7 5 4   │   N   │   Hearts :   Q J 6
Diamonds : Q 9 5 4 3   │ W   E │   Diamonds : K J 8 2
Clubs :   5   │   S   │   Clubs :   9 8
                       └───────┘
              Spades :   A K 9 3 2
              Hearts :   A K 9 8 2
              Diamonds : ———
              Clubs :   10 4 3
</pre>

No Score. South dealer. "One Spade"—
West passes—North "Three Clubs" (Forcing
Bid). East passes. South "Four Hearts" (Forc-
ing Bid). North "Five Clubs" East passes—
South "Six Clubs."

DECLARER SHOULD BEWARE

of drawing a card from the Dummy until he
has decided to play it. A quitted card is a played
card.

If Declarer plays out of turn or leads from
the wrong hand, he may not voluntarily withdraw
the card led; but if either opponent protests
before a fourth card has been played a lead must
be made from the correct hand and the cards
played to the trick are taken back and cannot be
treated as exposed cards.

There is no penalty if Declarer or Partner
exposes a card after the bidding has closed.

If Opponents lead out of wrong hand, Declarer
may treat the card as exposed, or call a lead
of a suit from the correct hand.

" SACRIFICE PENALTIES "

Rather than have opponents make first game,
accept a penalty of not more than 400.

To prevent opponents making second game,
accept a penalty of not more than 600.

A first game is preferable to receiving less than
400 points in penalties.

If opponents have one game, and you are sure

of making a game, refuse a penalty of less than 600 points.

CUTTING AND DEALING

In cutting, low wins, Ace counts low. Clubs rank lower than diamonds, and so on. Two lowest are partners. Lowest gets the deal, choice of cards, and seats. All must cut from same deck. Top and bottom four cards must not be cut.

LEADING TO A " NO-TRUMP " DECLARATION

Your partner not having bid, lead the fourth best of your longest suit. By " the rule of eleven " your partner will be able to locate nearly all the cards of that suit.

The exception to this lead is when holding a long suit headed by a high sequence, then lead top of sequence.

Having a long suit headed by Ace, Jack, Ten, or King, Jack, Ten, lead Jack.

Holding a long suit headed by Ace, King, and no re-entries, lead small one. Headed by Ace, King, Jack, lead Ace.

Leading an Ace calls for your partner's highest card of that suit.

Partner having bid, lead highest card of his suit. Unless you have four, then lead fourth best.

With a long suit in dummy, endeavour to exhaust the re-entry cards.

DISCARDING

Watch the discards. The discard of a six or better indicates strength ; if followed by a higher discard, weakness.

Discard of a two, three, four, or five indicates weakness, unless followed by a lower one, indicating strength.

Sometimes it is advisable to show weakness in two suits rather than shorten a strong defensive suit.

FALSE CARDING

When declarer, false card as much as possible.

When playing against declarer, do not mislead your partner.

ENCOURAGING CARDS

Ace or King lead, playing six or better, shows strength, always provided player had some option as to what card could be played.

[30]

HOLDING UP A HIGH CARD

Sometimes it is advisable to withhold a high card of a long suit in dummy, with the hope that declarer's hand will be exhausted of the suit and unable to get into dummy. This applies particularly to no trumps, or in a suit bid when trumps are exhausted.

In a no-trump bid, declarer will frequently withhold the commanding card of opponents' suit, until one opponent is exhausted.

PLAYING THE HAND

Decide on your plan of campaign before playing to the first trick.

It is often advisable to play a high card from the concealed hand and conserve dummy's re-entries.

The usual procedure is to immediately draw the trumps and establish a suit. Before drawing trumps, decide whether you can use dummy's trumps to trump a suit that dummy may be short of.

Having drawn trumps, proceed to set up your suits. Watch your opponents' discards for signals of strength or weakness, and finesse accordingly.

Do not finesse if unnecessary. First play your long suits.

Holding Ace, Jack in one hand and King, Ten in the other, leave this until opponents open it. You are then bound to make three tricks in that suit.

Holding Ace in one hand and Queen in the other—no other honours—never lead the Queen towards the Ace—opponents will cover the Queen and you will only make the Ace. Lead up to the Queen, if King is in second hand, you make two tricks.

POINTERS

DON'TS

With any kind of a hand, do not let your opponents get the contract too cheaply. They can frequently be driven into too high a bid.

If, by passing, you can leave your opponents in a non-game going hand, do so, unless you have a game going hand.

Don't look at your opponents' cards. It prevents you from claiming a revoke.

Don't emphasize a bid, pass, double, or play.

Don't hesitate in bidding.

Don't criticize your partner.

Don't call attention to the score.

Don't grumble at your luck.

Don't hold inquests.

Don't touch your cards during the deal. Fifty points penalty if you cause a card to be exposed.

Don't fidget when dummy. Watch the play and check up on opponents, particularly when they do not follow suit. Practise counting the cards and locating them in the various hands. When partner does not follow suit, ask if he has any, and in doing so emphasize the suit. "Failing in HEARTS."

Ascertain whether your partner opens the bidding with a four-card suit. If he still uses the antiquated five-card opening bid, your trump requirements to support partner's one bid may be reduced to three small or two with Queen or better, plus the same number of outside tricks as for a four-card suit bid.

It is pleasanter to follow his style than to correct; correcting starts arguments. Right or wrong, don't argue.

NOTE: No attempt has been made herein to cover the complete laws of Contract.

CONTRACT BRIDGE SCORES

No Trumps, 35; Spades and Hearts, 30; Diamonds and Clubs, 20.

Suits rank in order named. Two Spades being higher than two Hearts, etc.

Doubling doubles trick values and penalties. Redoubling doubles the double values.

Honours or Slam Premiums are not affected by doubling.

GAME is 100 points. Only tricks contracted for and made count towards game.

All extra tricks, premiums, and penalties are scored in the honour column. (Exception: Revoke penalty. For first revoke, 250 points are added to opponents' score, or alternatively, two tricks may be taken at the end of play from the revoking side and added to the tricks of opponents. They are figured as though actually won in play. Subsequent revokes in same hand are penalized 250 points each, and scored in the honour column.)

RUBBER is ended when one side has won two games.

After a side has won a game they are termed "VULNERABLE." Their penalties and bonuses are greatly increased.

HONOURS. FOUR in one hand, 100 points. FIVE in one hand, 150 points. FOUR ACES in one hand in No TRUMPS, 150 points. No other Honour scores.

PREMIUMS for winning two-game Rubber, 700 points. Three-game Rubber, 500 points. *unfinished rubber 300 for game won —*

FULFILLING CONTRACT. Not Vulnerable or Vulnerable. Undoubled, 0 points.

[37]

Doubled. Not Vulnerable, 50 points. Redoubled, 100 points. Doubled. Vulnerable, 100 points. Redoubled, 200 points.

SLAMS. Premiums ONLY COUNT when Slams are bid.

Small Slam. Not Vulnerable, 500 points. Vulnerable, 750 points.

Grand Slam. Not Vulnerable, 1000 points. Vulnerable, 1500 points.

OVERTRICKS. BONUS. Undoubled. Vulnerable or not, 50 points each trick. Doubled. Not Vulnerable. Each trick, 100 points. Redoubled, 200 points. Doubled and Vulnerable. Each trick, 200 points. Redoubled, 400 points.

PENALTIES FOR UNDERTRICKS

UNDOUBLED	Not Vulnerable	Vulnerable
First trick	50 points	100 points
Each subsequent trick	50 points	200 points

	Not Vulnerable		Vulnerable	
DOUBLED	Points	Total	Points	Total
First trick	100	100	200	200
Second trick	100	200	400	600
Third trick	200	400	400	1000
Fourth trick	200	600	400	1400
Fifth trick	400	1000	400	1800

[38]

| All subsequent tricks | All subsequent tricks |
| 400 points each | 400 points each. |

REDOUBLING doubles the above figures.

REVOKE PENALTIES

Penalty for first revoke : *Either* two tricks taken at end of hand and counted as though won in play, carrying Slam Premiums if bid, *or* 250 points.

Subsequent revokes same hand: 250 points each, scored in honour column.

N.B.—The offender and his partner cannot score any points won in the hand other than points for honours and infringements.

INDEX

	PAGE
Assisting Partner's Bid	8–11
Bidding	4– 6
Bidding Third Hand	6
Business Doubles	13, 22
Changing Partner's Bid	10
Cutting and Dealing	29
Discarding	30
Don'ts	35
Encouraging Cards	30
Example Hands	26–27
False Carding	30
Finessing	16
Forcing Take-out	10–11
Goulashes	24
Holding up a High Card	31
Informatory Double	12
Leading	14, 23, 28
Playing the Hand	31
Raising Partner's Bid	8, 11
Replying to Partner's Bid	8, 11
Replying to Informative Double	13
Revoke Penalties	39
Rule of Eleven	23
"Sacrifice Penalties"	28
Scores	36–38
Slam Bidding	21
Tricks Table	5
Two-Suited Hands	21
Unblocking	23
Vanderbilt	22